BUGS

Activity and Coloring Book

Fran Newman-D'Amico

DOVER PUBLICATIONS
Garden City, New York

This fun-filled book will take you into the busy, "buzzy" world of bugs. Whether you call them bugs or insects, you'll find that ants, grasshoppers, flies, and beetles are everywhere we go. Some bugs crawl, others fly, and many live in the ground, in trees, or even in houses and apartments! Many people think that spiders are insects (even though they're not), so they are included, too.

There are mazes, shape codes, crosswords, riddles, and connect-the-dots, as well as special pages just for you to design and color. Enjoy your visit to the world of the creepiest, crawliest creatures on earth!

Copyright

Copyright © 2007 by Dover Publications
All rights reserved.

Bibliographical Note

Bugs Activity and Coloring Book is a new work,
first published by Dover Publications in 2007.

International Standard Book Number

ISBN-13: 978-0-486-46199-1
ISBN-10: 0-486-46199-8

Manufactured in the United States of America
46199812   2023
www.doverpublications.com

Bee Buzz

I am called the Queen, even though I don't wear a crown!
Connect the dots from 1 to 29 to see my picture.

1

Moth Match

Did you know that moths like to fly at night? That's why you can see the moon in this picture. Look carefully at the moths. Find and circle the two moths that are exactly alike.

2

Tulip Time

Color Code

1 = green
2 = pink
3 = orange
4 = red
5 = blue
6 = yellow
7 = brown
8 = purple

The damselfly, grasshopper, and ant have all gathered to admire these beautiful tulips. Use the Color Code at the top of the page to color the picture—or choose your own colors.

3

Hide-and-Seek

Spot the bugs hidden in this garden. Find and circle
4 🐛, 5 🐞, 3 🦋, 2 🐝, 3 🐞, and 2 🦟 .

4

Name Game

+ **=** horsefly

+ **=** _____

+ **=** _____

+ **=** _____

+ **=** _____

Use each pair of pictures to make a new word that is the name of an insect. Write the name in the blank. The first pair has been done for you.

Wacky Web

```
H E S P I N E A L
L A T G N C W Z E
S P I D E R B W A
T N C N D A C E F
A W K E P W S B A
F L Y I B L A C K
```

WORD BOX

WEB	SPIN
SPIDER	LEAF
FLY	STICKY
BLACK	CRAWL

Find and circle the eight words in the Word Box
in the puzzle at the center of the web.

Ant Hill

This ant is on her way to meet a friend for a picnic lunch.
Please help her find the right path to take from Start to End.

Fun Facts

▲ = b ✏ = e ❁ = a ◆ = l

▢ = t ✳ = g ▮ = n ❋ = o

I can carry 50 times my weight.
Who am I?

___ ___ ___
❋ ▮ ▢

I can swim on my back and use
my legs as paddles.
Who am I?

___ ___ ___ ___ ___ ___ ___ ___ ___ ___ ___ ___ ___ ___
◆ ✳ ▮ ✳ ▲ ❋ ❁ ▢ ▲ ✏ ✏ ▢ ◆ ✏

To solve the riddles, use the shape code at the top of the
page. Write the letter that goes with each shape in the
spaces—and then answer the riddles!

Pond Playtime

This insect loves to fly over ponds and flutter its colorful wings. To see what it is, connect the dots from 1 to 34.

9

Plant Fun

These bugs are enjoying the sunshine as
they play in and around the flowerpot.

10

Plant Fun

The picture of the flowerpot and the playful bugs has changed.
Find and circle the five things that are different.

Word Fun

3. DOWN

1. ACROSS

| | I | | A | A |

| ³C | I | C | | T |

4. ACROSS

E

2. DOWN

| ⁴M | | | H | |

| | | P | I | | |
E

5. ACROSS

3. ACROSS

7. DOWN

6. ACROSS

| ⁶B | | E |

7. DOWN

This picture is just buzzing with activity! Fill in the names of
these tiny creatures where they belong in the puzzle.

Let's Go!

This happy frog just dropped by to see his friend. Find and circle his friend, who has two antennae, six legs, and four spots.

Bug Parts

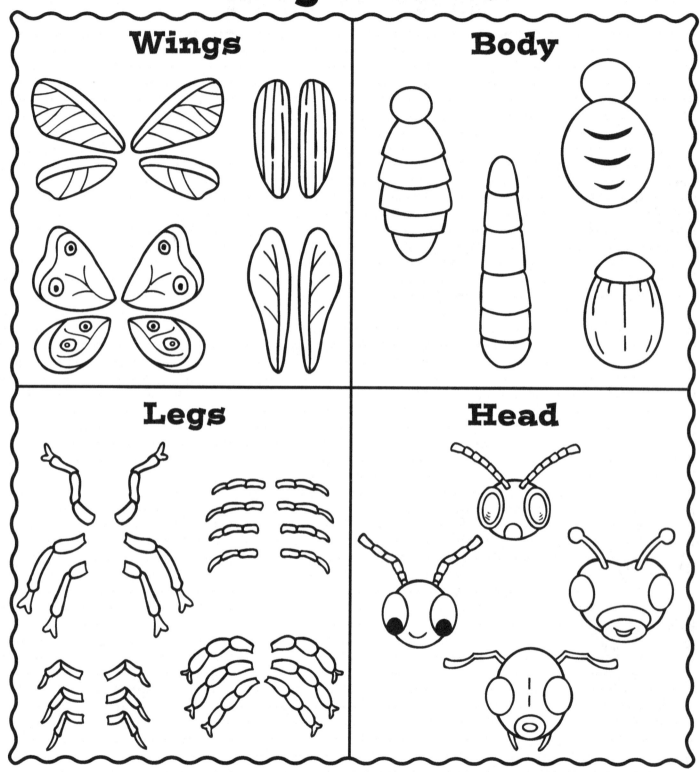

Wings

Body

Legs

Head

A bug's body is made of different parts. Pick one head, one body, some wings, and some legs and draw a picture of your very own bug on the facing page.

Create-a-Bug

Here's your bug!

Bug Scramble

What does grasshopper love to do?

POH

__ __ __

How does wasp travel the sky?

LFY

__ __ __

What sound does bee make?

ZUZB

__ __ __ __

How does flea land on his friends?

PJMU

__ __ __ __

Each group of letters spells a word. Answer the questions by unscrambling the letters and writing the words in the blanks.

Busy Bugs

The flowers are in bloom, and these bugs couldn't be happier!
Look carefully and circle the two bugs that are exactly alike.

Butterfly Beauty

Draw your own designs on the wings of this butterfly.
One wing has been done for you.

More Fun Facts

= a   ❖ = f   ✏ = u   ✺ = e   ▲ = l   ◆ = o

● = h   ✳ = b   ❋ = y   ✿ = t   ▢ = r   ✱ = c

I can taste with my feet.
Who am I?

_____

✱ ✏ ✿ ✿ ✺ ▢ ❖ ▲ ✱

I can live up to 9 days without my head.
Who am I?

_____

▢ ◆ # ✱ ●

To solve the riddles, use the shape code at the top of
the page. Write the letter that goes with each shape in
the spaces—and then answer the riddles!

Sky-Lighters

Jason loves lightning bugs! Are there more bugs inside the jar, or in the sky? Write the number of bugs inside the jar on the lid. Write the number of bugs in the sky inside the moon.

Bug Match

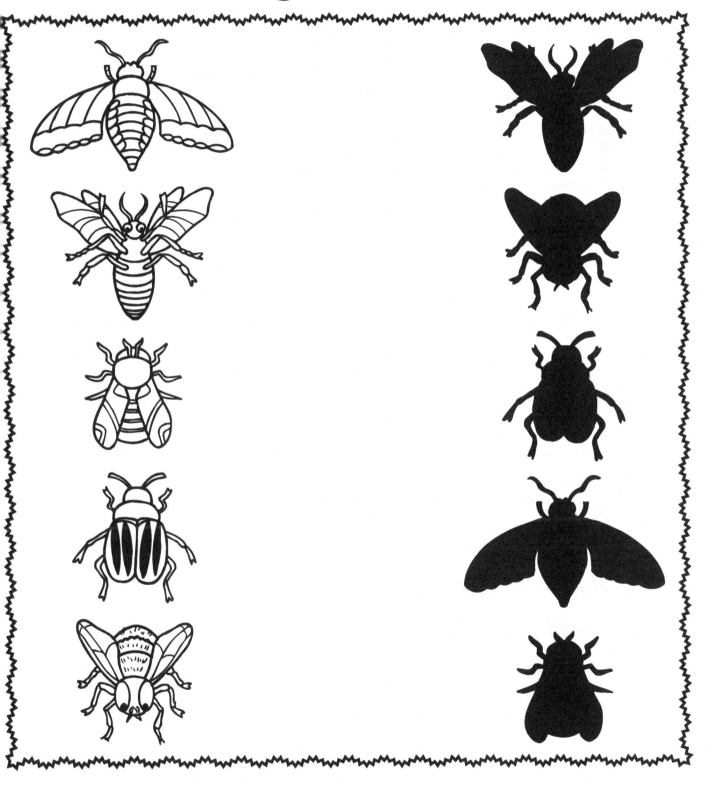

The bugs on this page are shown with their shadows. Draw a line from each bug on the left to its shadow on the right.

Ladybug Math

Color the ladybugs on the left yellow.
Color the ladybugs on the right red.
Draw 3 spots on each ladybug.
Draw 6 legs on each ladybug.

1. How many ladybugs did you color yellow? _____

2. How many ladybugs did you color red? _____

3. How many ladybugs did you color all together? _____

4. How many legs did you draw in total? _____

5. How many spots did you draw in total? _____

Follow the directions to color and draw the ladybugs on this page.
Then answer the five questions below them.

Picture Search

Look at the pictures above carefully. Find the 2 sets of pictures below that match the same order. Look up and down and across.

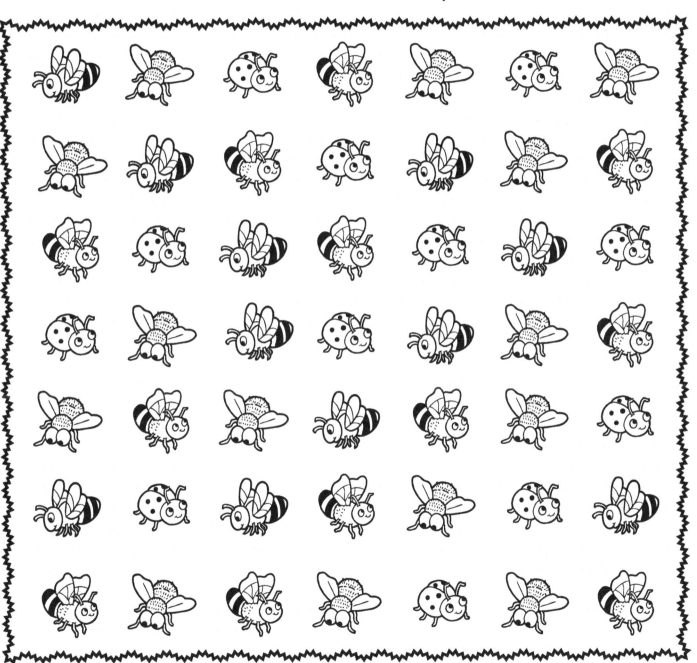

Creepy, Crawly...

I start out in life crawling. I creep over leaves and inch my way up trees. Who am I?

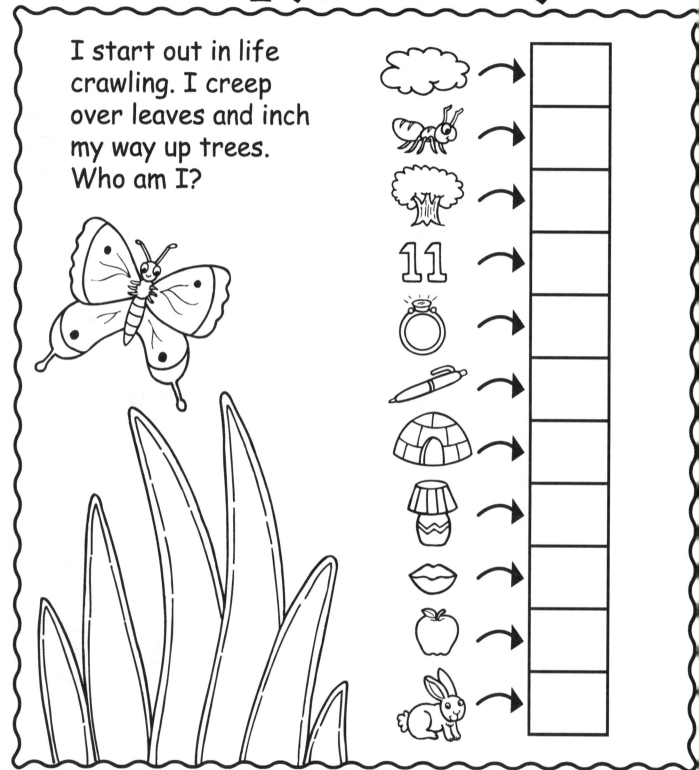

Use the picture clues to find out the answer to the question. Write the first letter of each picture in a box. Then read the word you have spelled—there's your answer!

Garden Secrets

Believe it or not, the word BUG appears six times in this garden!
Look carefully and circle the words. Good luck!

Solutions

Bee Buzz

page 1

Moth Match

page 2

Hide-and-Seek

page 4

Name Game

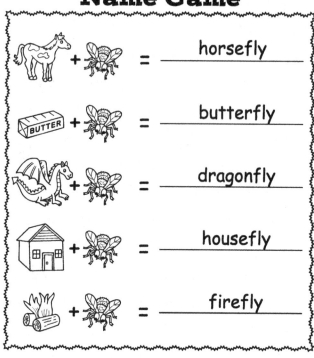

page 5

Wacky Web

WORD BOX

WEB	SPIN
SPIDER	LEAF
FLY	STICKY
BLACK	CRAWL

page 6

Ant Hill

End

Start

page 7

Fun Facts

▲=b ✏=e ✹=a ❖=l

▢=t ❋=g ▮=n ✳=o

I can carry 50 times my weight.
Who am I?

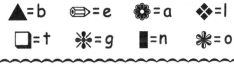

a n t
✹ ▮ ▢

I can swim on my back and use
my legs as paddles.
Who am I?

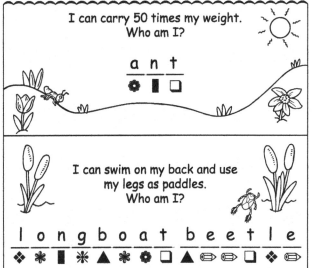

l o n g b o a t b e e t l e
❖ ✳ ▮ ❋ ▲ ✳ ✹ ▢ ▲ ✏ ✏ ▢ ❖ ✏

page 8

Pond Playtime

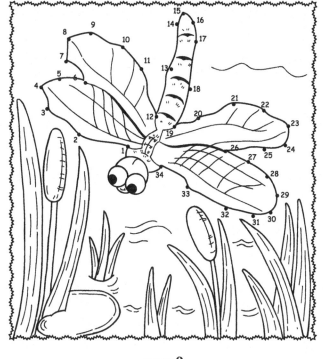

page 9

Plant Fun

page 11

Word Fun

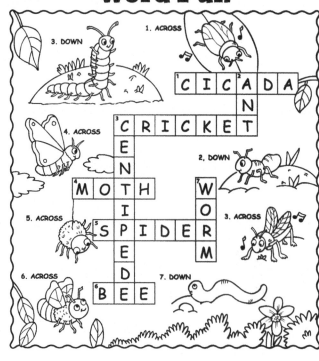

page 12

Let's Go!

page 13

Bug Scramble

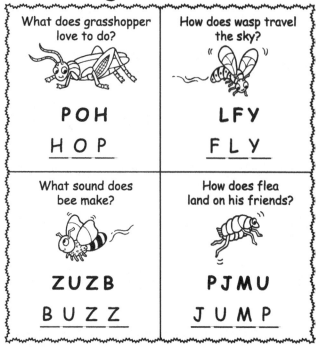

page 16

Busy Bugs

page 17

More Fun Facts

= a ◆ = f ✏ = u ◎ = e ▲ = l ◆ = o
● = h ✳ = b ✴ = y ✿ = t ▢ = r ✱ = c

page 19

Sky-Lighters

page 20

Bug Match

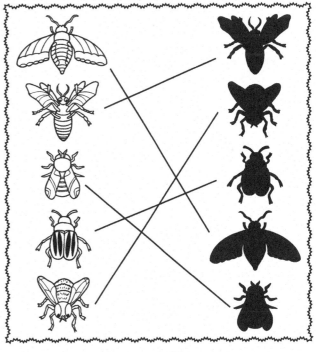

page 21

Ladybug Math

Color the ladybugs on the left yellow.
Color the ladybugs on the right red.
Draw 3 spots on each ladybug.
Draw 6 legs on each ladybug.

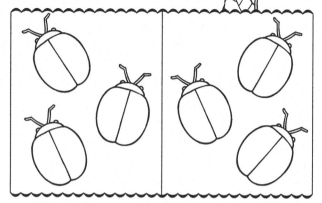

1. How many ladybugs did you color yellow? __3__
2. How many ladybugs did you color red? __3__
3. How many ladybugs did you color all together? __6__
4. How many legs did you draw in total? __36__
5. How many spots did you draw in total? __18__

page 22

Picture Search

Look at the pictures above carefully. Find the 2 sets of pictures below that match the same order. Look up and down and across.

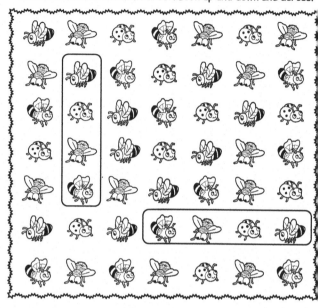

page 23

Creepy, Crawly...

I start out in life crawling. I creep over leaves and inch my way up trees. Who am I?

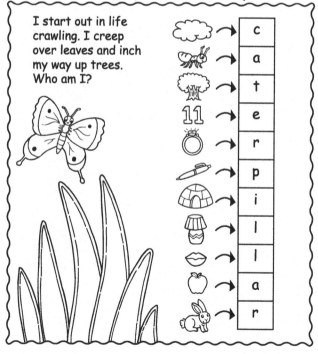

c
a
t
e
r
p
i
l
l
a
r

page 24

Garden Secrets

page 25

30